Historic Public Parks
BRISTOL

Historic Public Parks

BRISTOL

David Lambert

Avon Gardens Trust
in association with Bristol City Council

First published in 2000 by
Avon Gardens Trust
The CREATE Centre, Smeaton Road, Bristol BS1 6XN
Registered Charity Number: 900377

*We are very grateful to the Bristol Reference Library, the City Museum
and Art Gallery, Bristol Record Office and Bygone Bristol postcards, for
permission to publish illustrations from their collections. While postcards are
a familiar source of information on parks, Bristol is fortunate in having a
unique resource in the form of the drawings of Samuel Loxton (1857-1922)
who, in the first decade of the twentieth century, produced thousands
of topographical drawings for the* Bristol Observer *and* Bristol
Evening News, *now deposited in the Reference Library.*

ISBN 0 9531013 2 0

Designed by Martin Burnham (0117) 9550054
Printed in England by Burleigh Press, Bristol BS2 0YA

CONTENTS

PREFACE

*'a measure of a city's greatness
is to be found in the quality of its public
spaces, its parks and squares.'*

John Ruskin

This statement is as relevant today as it was when it was written over a century ago. Public parks are much-needed green lungs, vital open spaces amongst ever-spreading development in towns and cities. They are also an important part of the nation's heritage, although in many places they are suffering from shortage of funding.

World War II began an unfortunate period of decline for parks, when miles of railings, gates and other features were removed allegedly 'to help the war effort' and, more reasonably, areas were converted to growing food. In the following years, Councils' chief need for money was for housing. With little to spare for park maintenance and supervision, neglect and lack of security led to an increase in vandalism, requiring more money for repair work which was not forthcoming - a downward spiral.

The situation is at last improving. Nationally, the Urban Parks section of the Heritage Lottery Fund has contributed large sums to a programme of improvement and the condition of 'the environment' has become a topic of more general concern. Bristol is fortunate in now having a good proportion of public green space, though this was not always so. In the nineteenth century, when the city was less prosperous than in its earlier heyday, the Corporation was generally reluctant to provide public parks. In the latter part of the twentieth century the City Council has been enlightened enough to buy for public use what were once great private estates: Ashton Court, Oldbury Court, Blaise Castle, Kingsweston. Unfortunately, the need for maintenance in these larger areas has tended to divert attention and resources from the smaller public parks within the city.

These neighbourhood parks are well-loved by local people and tourists and they make a valuable contribution to Bristol's heritage. There are features in these parks which are in need of conservation and restoration, and the parks as a whole need sympathetic management before it is too late to save their essential character. Bristol is developing a network of local park groups who work with the council on a range of projects that include practical conservation and the improvement of facilities, such as children's play areas. There is also a Parks Panel, a forum for discussion, which includes representatives from the groups, along with others from interested organisations such as the Civic Society, Wildlife Trust and Avon Gardens Trust.

This book is the third in a series covering the historic public parks of Bristol, Bath and Weston-super-Mare. The aim of the series is to help local people and visitors appreciate the great resource public parks represent. David Lambert, the author of this volume, is Conservation Officer for the Garden History Society, and as a result he has a wide knowledge of parks and gardens all over the country. He was a founder member of the Avon Gardens Trust and has been in turn its Secretary, Chairman and Conservation Officer. He is a distinguished and well-known garden historian and lecturer, author of several books and reports. David is a member of the Heritage Lottery Fund expert panel on Public Parks and he was one of the advisers to the House of Commons Environment Committee's recent Inquiry into Town and Country Parks.

In this book David Lambert relates the story of the gradual development in the nineteenth and twentieth centuries of several of the public open spaces created and managed by the local authority, the original 'people's parks', but not the history of the former private estates or the town squares which need volumes to themselves.

The series of books on historic public parks was initiated by the Avon Gardens Trust, originally in association with the former Avon Planning Department, and now with the Councils of Bristol City, Bath & North East Somerset, and North Somerset. This volume on Bristol Parks has been funded by the Avon Gardens Trust with a contribution from Bristol City Council.

Peggy Stembridge
Chairman, Avon Gardens Trust
May 2000

INTRODUCTION

Bristol can boast, with a reasonable degree of confidence if not absolute certainty, of the oldest public open space in the country. Brandon Hill was granted to the Corporation in 1174 by the Earl of Gloucester. Despite this honourable precedent, Bristol's record in creating urban parks since the twelfth century has been generally uninspiring until large former private estates were bought for public use in the twentieth century. The principal public open space in the crowded seventeenth-century city was the open land south of King Street known as the Marsh (Fig.1). This was much-used as a public resort, laid out with shady walks and popular for bowls, bear-baiting and fireworks, although this was not considered when the Corporation decided to use the land to build a grand new Square, Queen Square, begun in 1699.

After the loss of the Marsh, College Green continued to offer a public amenity, but its condition was often a matter of public complaint. In the seventeenth century, it was recorded as 'in a scandalous condition, being ploughed up by the sledges carrying clothes to dry on Brandon Hill', and used even on Sundays for huge disorderly games of 'stop-ball'. After the Great Storm of 1703 it was levelled and beautified and a new avenue planted but by 1756 it was again neglected,

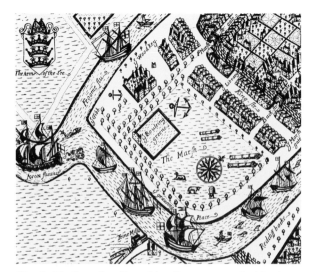

Fig. 1 *The formal walks and bowling green on the Marsh, as recorded on Millerd's 1673 map of Bristol.*

and neighbours put together the money to restore the turf and walks, eventually pressuring the Cathedral into a small contribution. These repairs were the occasion for the removal of Bristol's High Cross, apparently after lobbying by leading citizens because its location at the intersection of the walks 'prevented parties of promenaders from walking abreast, and was often defiled by nuisances'. The cross was given by the Dean and Chapter to Henry Hoare of Stourhead in Wiltshire where it still stands. A copy was reinstated by public subscription in 1850 (Fig. 2).

Fig. 2 *An early twentieth-century view of College Green, with the copy of the Bristol Cross erected after the original had been removed to Stourhead.*

In the later eighteenth and early nineteenth century, a number of the new squares offered some public access: apart from Queen Square, King Square, Portland and Brunswick Squares all were referred to as places of public recreation (Fig. 3). But this may have been limited, and certainly later squares - such as Victoria Square in Clifton - were generally restricted to access by the neighbouring householders.

The most important garden open to the public, although not publicly owned, was the Bristol and Clifton Zoological Gardens which were opened in 1836. Although now the landscaping is designed quite properly as much for the benefit of the animals as for the visitors, the original design by Richard Forrest laid great emphasis on the botanical quality and variety of the plants and their public display (Fig. 4).

The development of Bristol's urban parks in the nineteenth century was a slow business, the City lagging well behind the great northern and midland industrial towns. Despite its pretensions to being still the second city, Bristol's economy had stagnated throughout what were boom years further north and the urban expansion which fuelled park development elsewhere did not happen in Bristol. In addition, there was not the influx of new private wealth which expanding manufacturing industries created elsewhere. Finally, there seems to have been a long tradition of parsimony on the part of City fathers (the Council, the Merchant Venturers etc.), bound up with mercantile good sense. When the parks movement did begin in Bristol, it was never driven by a Council determined to leave its mark, but rather by pressure in the 1870s and 80s from working class organisations and liberals (industrialists, MPs, clergymen) over the chronic housing problems which Bristol suffered from the 1850s onward.

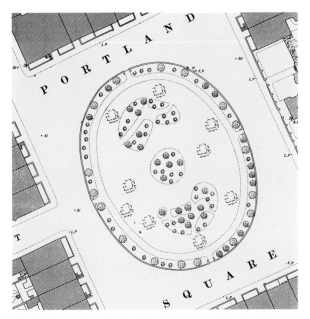

Fig. 3 *The garden in Portland Square as recorded by the Ordnance Survey in 1884.*

In evidence to a Government inspector's inquiry into the Corporation's improvement scheme of 1847, the Town Clerk itemised the city's places of public recreation: Queen Square (Fig. 5) had over $6^3/_4$ acres, College Green about $4^1/_2$ acres, Brunswick Square $1^1/_4$ acre, Portland Square $2^1/_4$ acres, and King Square nearly $1^1/_4$ acre; Brandon Hill was $19^1/_2$ acres. This rather feeble list was obviously no great cause of civic

Fig. 4 The Zoological Gardens in the early twentieth century.

embarrassment, because - the Downs Act of 1861 aside - nothing was done for another thirty or forty years.

In 1850 Bristol was the third most unhealthy city in England. Sir H T de la Beche and Dr Lyon Playfair in their *Report on the Sanitary Condition of Bristol* (1845) criticised the defective state of public services, especially sewerage and water systems, the inadequacy of the latter having little comparison in the whole of England. Bristol did nothing to address the critical problem of housing, although it did adopt the 1848 Public Health Act and set up a Sanitary Committee in 1851, as well as appointing a Medical Officer of Health. As a result, widespread concern about working class housing only developed in the 1880s when it

was a national issue, and only in 1890 was a Bristol Committee for Promoting the Better Housing of the Poor set up by councillors and philanthropists.

In 1858, Matthews' *New History of Bristol* boasted of the city's 'public parades and ... agreeable places to walk on', and referred to the Hotwells Colonade, and the walk by the river, the parade near Dowry Square and the Mall in Clifton; while in the city itself there were the gravel walk on Brandon Hill, College Green, and Queen Square, a river-side walk behind Bridge Street, St James's Churchyard, a parade on Kingsdown, Brunswick Square and King Square,

Fig. 5 Queen Square as depicted by Thomas Rowbotham in 1827.
[Bristol Museum and Art Gallery]

Redcliff Churchyard and Redcliff Parade. However, these were either urban squares or gravel walks, and at that date there was still no people's park of the kind being developed elsewhere.

Bristol's first move towards provision of public open space on a significant scale was its acquisition of public rights over the Downs from the Lords of the Manor of Henbury and the Society of Merchant Venturers. By purchasing land at Henbury, the Council had acquired the rights of commoners; this was followed by their buying out the rights of the Lords of the Manor with the Merchant Venturers surrendering their rights voluntarily. The Clifton and Durdham Downs (Bristol) Act 1861 established free access and the move was widely welcomed. As a *Bristol Times and Mirror* report (16 May 1865) remarked 'The Downs are now the People's Park'.

The 1861 Act created a new Downs Committee which had its first meeting in November of that year. It oversaw many improvements chiefly in the 1870s: new seats, drainage, the filling-in of old quarries, and a new carriage drive round the Downs completed in 1877, which added 'to the enjoyment, without in any way destroying the picturesque beauty, of the Downs'. A report of 1879 refers to 'planting trees, re-gravelling walks, repairing ... seats' without 'altering (the Downs') undulating surface or rural features which form so

Fig. 6 The Downs' 'undulating surface and rural features' in the early twentieth century.

attractive a part of the scenery'(Fig. 6). Alderman Proctor left a legacy of £100 to the Committee to be used to erect the grandiose drinking-fountain named after him and still standing near the end of the Promenade on the Downs.

The Committee's aim was 'preserving the Downs as a place of enjoyable resort and recreation for the public', but the proposition that the Downs functioned as a 'people's park' was demonstrably absurd. The catchment area was the wealthiest area of Bristol, a correspondent to the *Bristol Times and Mirror* (19 April 1865) sought to reassure the local residents, pointing out that 'The long day's "recreation" is often too much for those who are used to the quiet of regular work'.

In terms of historical records, the first great rallying call for a genuine people's park is *The Cry of the Poor, being a letter from Sixteen Working Men of Bristol to the Sixteen Aldermen of the City,* dated November 1871 (Fig. 7). This pamphlet addressed several demands, including a free lending library and newsrooms and a free bathing pool. Of the need for a park, it compared Bristol to 'nearly all the great towns of the North' which had such 'lungs of great cities'. 'You will say we have Clifton and Durdham Downs, but these are mainly for rich people who can afford to live in that neighbourhood: it would take us an hour's walking, after the hard toil of the day is over, to get to these beautiful spots, and then another hour to get home, thus making pleasure a toil.' Despite its eloquence, it produced no results.

In 1875 the new Public Health Act gave local authorities the power to raise loans from central government for the purpose of acquiring or improving land for recreation and on 26 May that year the *Western Daily Press* tried to resurrect the issue with an editorial headed 'A Public Park for St Philips', trying to shame the Council into action: 'A wealthy city should consider these open spaces as necessary as public roads'.

Then in a speech to the Council meeting of 26 June 1877, the Liberal MP Lewis Fry urged that land at Stapleton, which Sir John Greville Smyth was offering for sale, be bought for a public park, citing public health reasons

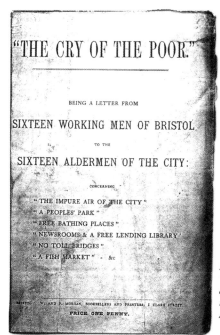

Fig. 7
'The Cry of the Poor': a publication largely ignored by the Aldermen addressed.

and pointing to the example of Liverpool, Manchester and Leeds where parks had been laid out. In July, the City's Land Steward inspected the land and reported enthusiastically but the Council hesitated over the condition that it be dedicated in perpetuity as open space, and also over Smyth's asking price. And there things remained for another ten years. However, the issue was creeping up the political agenda.

On 19 May 1881 the Town Council asked the Committee responsible for health and open spaces, the Sanitary Committee, to take forward the Council's resolution on 'the desirability of securing any open sites that may be available in the crowded parts of the city and planting trees and placing seats thereon'. The Committee suggested St James's Churchyard might be the first candidate, and it also suggested that suitable sites should be sought in St Philips and Bedminster.

Around this time a number of parishes (Temple, St Nicholas, St James's) began converting redundant burial grounds into public gardens, which the Council was able to encourage under the terms of the Metropolitan Open Spaces Act 1881 (Fig. 8). In 1882, the Council also inspected a parcel of land off Newfoundland Road (later St Agnes Park) but concluded that it would probably cost too much to buy. It looked too at the burial ground between Redcross Street and the Frome or at least, grudgingly, 'that part of it which is not required for street improvements' and decided that it could 'with great advantage be converted into an open space or Play-ground for the inhabitants of that poor and populous neighbourhood', and this eventually became St Matthias Park, hemmed in by a tannery, an iron works and a malthouse (Fig. 9).

Although Cotham Gardens had been laid out in 1880 after a gift of land from the Fry family, the first real

Fig. 8 Church of St Philip and St Jacob: an early postcard showing the newly laid out public garden on the site of the former burial ground.

breakthrough came in 1882, when Sir John Greville Smyth offered 21½ acres by the river in Bedminster for a park. It was accepted the next year and 'The People's Park Bedminster' came into being (later to be renamed Greville Smyth Park). On 18 September 1884, hedged round with complaints that it was being asked to respond to political pressure for more open spaces, but then being criticised when its proposals necessitated higher rates, the Sanitary Committee reported on eight possible projects, including Bedminster (later Greville Smyth), St Matthias, and Cotham Gardens, as well as the lands which would eventually become Mina Road Park and Eastville Park. The provision of people's parks was finally underway.

Fig. 9 St Matthias Park in the early twentieth century: thirteen years after 'The Cry of the Poor', this tiny public garden was one of the few achievements of which the Corporation could boast.
[Bristol Reference Library]

Over the next ten to fifteen years, most of Bristol's parks were acquired and laid out. With some honourable exceptions, they illustrate an undistinguished history and some terrible missed opportunities: in 1884 for example the Council turned down the gift of the Arno's Vale estate after which the southern part was sold off for housing, leaving the Council to acquire the rump some 60 years later. There is no great central park to compare to Royal Victoria Park in Bath, none of the leading landscape architects was involved, and the design quality as a result is unexceptional.

Nevertheless, even the standard Victorian park is now a valuable local resource. Their history and evolution is intimately bound up with that of the City, and reflects it faithfully; they have been much loved parts of the local scene and although their condition has declined in the last twenty years, their importance is beginning to be recognised.

Bristol's urban parks, like so many, have suffered dreadfully in the last fifty years. In the last twenty, central Government has demanded savings, and parks have borne more than their fair share: the bandstand in the Dame Emily Smyth Playground was taken down in the mid-1990s; a characterful little shelter in Greville Smyth was demolished at about the same time; the vandalised Edwardian shelter in Fishponds Park was only demolished in January 2000. A replacement is to be provided housing an electricity sub-station. Encouragingly, the Council has recently carried out repairs to the attractive but unused little gardener's store in St James's Churchyard. The statue of Samuel Morley, the one reminder of the public garden which once occupied the Haymarket, has been moved to make way for the sail-like object at the entrance to Broadmead.

Built features within the parks have largely been removed or demolished. Bristol's record on this is particularly depressing. It is incredible that in a city the size of Bristol, no historic bandstands survive: they were not only amenities for practical use, shelters and meeting places as well as performance areas, but were great architectural focal points in the landscape (Fig. 10). Drinking fountains similarly were much more than functional objects; they had ornamental quality and often had memorial or exhortatory functions as well. One good example survives in Canford Park, but again, most have been demolished. Some were built specially in stone (Victoria Park), others were off-the-shelf cast-iron models selected from catalogues (as in Eastville and St George Parks) (Fig. 11). The Crimean cannons in Eastville, St George and Victoria Parks were all taken for scrap along with the railings during the Second World War, and whatever their associations they are missed as focal points and incidents for visitors. Similarly regrettable is the removal of much of the local oolitic limestone which made the rockeries in St Agnes Park or Fishponds Park (Fig. 12).

Any account of the history of Bristol's parks quickly undermines the legend of selfless millionaire philanthropists and noble, visionary aldermen such as those who were benefactors in some northern industrial cities. Instead, a picture emerges of stuttering progress with a dilatory Council, hard-bargaining landowners and grudging ratepayers on the one hand, and determined public campaigners, both working-class and middle-class, on the other.

Fig. 10 *The bandstand in St George Park.*

Between these two forces for progress and for inertia, we find - in fragmentary hints and glimpses - shadows of the gardeners and park-keepers who made the parks great and received scant reward, like the first keeper at St George Park, Robert Clements. Clements was paid 21 shillings per week for five twelve-hour days (ten at the weekend with alternate Sundays off). For the first six months he did not even have a shelter and incredibly had to wait for a Committee debate before he was allowed to wear his Fire Brigade overcoat to keep warm in the winter of 1896. This compared to the £800 per annum plus expenses being paid to the

Fig. 11 The lower entrance to Eastville Park, lost to the M32, showing the typical cast-iron drinking fountain.

Authority's Surveyor, Frederick Ashmead, in 1894. The caretaker at St Agnes even had to petition for Sunday afternoons off, while the caretakers at St Matthias, Cotham, Greville Smyth and Mina Road parks, were required to replace any dead tree or shrub out of their own wages. This insight into conditions comes from the 1889 notebook of the City Forester, Samuel Edward Cockbill (Fig. 13).

However, in the twentieth century, the City has had a commendable record in acquiring private estates for public use: Blaise Castle was bought in 1926, Oldbury Court in 1937, Arno's Vale in 1948, Ashton Court in

1959 and Kingsweston as recently as 1996. In the mid-1960s it was laudably decided not to redevelop the flattened heart of the city but instead to create a new park around the ruins of the castle and the blitzed shell of St Peter's Church. Castle Park was not laid out to the elaborate plans of Sir Hugh Casson's practice which included a palm house, herb and water garden and avenue, but it has nevertheless become a well-loved public open space. For these achievements, the City deserves great praise even if its subsequent management of these sites has been erratic in quality.

There are welcome signs that parks are now moving up the pecking order within the Leisure Services Department. The Department has secured grants for

Fig. 12 An early view of Fishponds Park, showing the kind of rockeries typical of the city parks when first laid out, and now almost entirely removed.

Blaise Castle and Ashton Court from the Heritage Lottery Fund, although its application for St Agnes Park was turned down. Recently gathered statistics have added weight to the claims for additional funding: in 1998/9 there were over 16 million visits to parks in Bristol, and parks were voted the second most important Council service. Public pressure is resulting in repair of features such as playgrounds, often paid for in part by local fund-raising campaigns, as at Dame Emily Smyth Playground. The Council as a whole is beginning to recognise the added value that parks give to the City's environment and amenities.

This little book cannot give a history and description of every public park in the City; although each one has a different story, there are too many. Instead, it will focus on a selection which illustrate the story of the parks movement in Bristol as a whole, and in so doing remind Bristol's citizens of their heritage - for it is genuinely a people's heritage - of how it was fought for and how it needs to be fought for still, so that it can be handed on to future generations in better condition than we find it today.

The descriptions are arranged in roughly chronological order, although in some cases acquisition, laying out and opening were spread over several years. The parks selected include the principal and largest parks as well as others which illustrate the range of Bristol's parks.

Fig. 13
Samuel Edward Cockbill,
City Forester during the main
period of park-building in Bristol.   *[Bristol Record Office]*

BRISTOL

1	Brandon Hill
2	Cotham Gardens
3	St James's Churchyard
4	Greville Smyth Park
5	Mina Road Park
6	St Agnes Park
7	Eastville Park
8	Victoria Park
9	St Andrew's Park
10	St George Park

THE DOWNS

REDLAND

ASHLEY DOWN

9

MONTPELIER

2

COTHAM

CLIFTON

ST.WERBURGH'S

5

6

EASTVILLE

7

WHITEHALL

EASTON

10

ST. GEORGE

ST. PAUL'S

3

CENTRE

REDFIELD

1

HOTWELLS

THE DINGS

BARTON HILL

ST. ANNE'S

4

SOUTHVILLE

ST. PHILIP'S MARSH

8

BEDMINSTER

WINDMILL HILL

ARNO'S VALE

0 ¼ ½ m

N

© 2000 Bristol City Council

BRANDON HILL

Nuisances and improvements

Brandon Hill may well be the oldest municipal open space in the country. All but the top four acres was granted to the Corporation in 1174 by Robert Earl of Gloucester. Initially sub-let to farmers, from 1625 it has been in the control of the Corporation: a public open space used for grazing and hay-making, for drying of clothes, for public meetings, and, since it was open for many years before bye-laws were prepared, for everything that comes under the heading of recreation.

During the Civil War, Brandon Hill was a key point in the defence of the city. A fort was built and substantial earthworks were constructed, probably in early 1643, against the advancing Royalist forces who attacked on 23 July 1643. The remains are most prominent to the west and south of Cabot Tower.

Although the space was public, it was not until the later nineteenth century that the boundaries were stabilised. During the early nineteenth century areas were nibbled off, for example to make a garden enclosure at the end of Great George Street for the Mansion House.

Fig. 15 Rowbotham and Muller's print of the Grand Reform Dinner on Brandon Hill, 1832. [Bristol City Museum and Art Gallery]

The character too of the hill was unstable, even volatile, until the mid-nineteenth century. Thomas Rowbotham and William Muller produced a print of a riotous rally on Brandon Hill, 'The Grand Reform Dinner on Brandon Hill' in August 1832. (Fig. 15) The hill was second only to Queen Square as a popular venue for public meetings, which in the late eighteenth and early nineteenth century were viewed with increasing hostility by the authorities. In the wake of the Bristol Riots, and in the 1830s, the heyday of Chartism, there was great antagonism between Chartists wishing to exercise an unimpeded right of assembly and free speech, and the Corporation's police force, with its station strategically built at the foot of the hill, now the headquarters of the Avon

Fig. 16 Cabot Tower, before the gardens were laid out at its foot.

Wildlife Trust. Residents of the large houses on Queen's Parade fronting the hill petitioned the City in January 1840 about 'nuisances' and asked for an increased police presence on the hill. Around that date, the Corporation began 'improvements' to Brandon Hill, and it is hard not to see these as a strategy against radicalism and working class organisation, dependent as both were on the large central open space.

The main feature of these mid-nineteenth century improvements was the terraced walk round the south side of the hill, which was probably started in 1839. In 1845, as residential development began to encroach, a subscription fund was started to make walks and walls and to ensure the hill's preservation as open space. In his evidence to the Government inquiry into the Corporation's improvement scheme of 1847, the Town Clerk stated of Brandon Hill that it was by far the largest recreational open space in the town at $19\frac{1}{2}$ acres and that £800 had been recently collected by private subscription for the purpose of forming public walks there.

The improvements included the mounting of two captured Russian guns on the summit on 19 August 1857. By 1858, Matthews' *New History of Bristol* refers to 'the gravel walk on Brandon Hill', as one of the amenities of the city. Despite the improvements and the gentrification, the hill continued as a venue for major events: 30,000 gathered there to witness the

Fig. 17 Samuel Loxton's view of Brandon Hill, little changed today, characterised still by roughly mown grass and wild flowers.
[Bristol Reference Library]

launch of SS Great Britain on 7 July 1843 and on 18 July 1874 there was a major agricultural labourers' demonstration on the hill. It is alarming to note that as late as 16 August 1892 boys caught throwing stones on Brandon Hill could be fined 5 shillings plus costs or sent to prison for seven days.

The wondrous, unruly Cabot Tower was built 1897-98 to a design by the eccentric Gothic architect, William Venn Gough, to mark the occasion of the 400th anniversary of Cabot's 'discovery' of America (Fig.16).

It became the focal point of a new garden element in the public open space, when the Sanitary Committee, which had taken over responsibility for the hill in 1924, authorised the construction of 'alpine and water gardens, pools and waterfalls' during 1936-37. In 1949-50, a new heather garden was made at the base of the Tower. The Tower dominates the hill, but remarkably the hill itself still retains some of the air of rough grazing land in the heart of a metropolis which must always have been its character, a character now being enhanced by the Avon Wildlife Trust's management (Fig.17).

The lower slopes above Jacob's Wells Road, accessed by a series of Pennant steps, are dense with scrub, which obscures some dramatic natural rock and artificial rockwork. The lower walk, on the line of the old footpath from Clifton to the City, curving round to Brandon Steep, is planted with Limes. The railings around Brandon Hill, contemporary with the Pennant retaining walls, are generally about three feet high, although at the end of Great George Street, which is lined with Plane and Lime, there are gates and flanking spear-headed railings in a much more imposing style. The main terrace walk remains an imposing feature, now surfaced with asphalt, with a cobbled gutter on the upper side. There is an attractive, thirties-style gardener's store in brick and pebble-dash with tiled roof by the works compound. On the southern slopes, there is a fine drinking fountain set in a rugged Pennant embrasure, backed by Holly and other shrubs and a wrought-iron railing. There are various types of benches scattered over the hill, including a fine circular seat around an Oak.

The ornamental gardens are very attractive, despite not quite being on the scale of Gough's Tower or the wider landscape. They are laid out around two irregular ponds, concrete-lined and surrounded with rockery work, with a central cascade from the base of the Tower, falling through channels into one of the ponds. The gardens are planted with a mixture of dwarf evergreens, Cypress and Juniper, and flowering shrubs, and crazy-paving paths, typical of the period, are edged in places by low hooped railings.

The gardens aside, the planting on Brandon Hill is a typical parkland mix of Limes, London Plane and Oak, with the occasional Beech and Holm Oak, e.g. on the slope between Charlotte Street South and Great George Street. Limes are planted along not only the southern walk but also on sections of the main terrace walk further up the slope. There is a very fine Oak in the works compound just beneath the Tower, and a memorial Oak of 1869 on the Civil War earthworks.

There are several historically interesting notices and signs around Brandon Hill: a hand-painted wooden sign warning about damaging turf and quoting the bye-law on times for carpet-beating to the south of the Great George Street entrance; a pressed metal sign near the lower pond reminding users of others' enjoyment and requesting us not to litter; a sign attached to the circular iron bench around the memorial Oak planted in 1869 by the Mayoress to commemorate the marriage of the Prince of Wales; and a similar sign commemorating the oak planted in 1902 to mark the coronation of Edward VII.

COTHAM GARDENS

'A beautiful little pleasure-ground adjoining Lovers' walk'

Cotham Gardens was one of the first public gardens created in the city. A thousand-year lease on 4³/₄ acres of the Cotham Tower estate was granted to the City by members of the Fry family and others in 1879, for a shilling a year. The lease also included part of the avenue of Redland Court, and it is interesting to note that the Local Board of Health on agreeing to proceed with the conveyance thanked not only Francis Fry and the other owners but also 'the subscribers to the fund for preserving the Avenue'. The Frys' gift was augmented by a gift of land from the trustees of the banker, George Edwards of Redland Court who gave the City the lower part of Redland Grove in 1884.

Having secured the land, members of the Corporation visited the site in 1880 and ordered that firstly the grass should be cut, secondly 'that the whole of the land be fenced in' and thirdly that the Surveyor prepare a plan. On 20 April 1881, 'a beautiful little

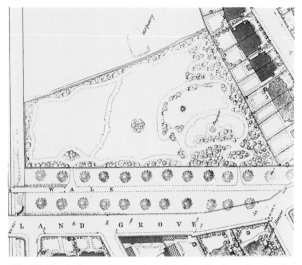

Fig. 18 *The Ordnance Survey plan of Cotham Gardens showing the elaborate shrubbery walks, 1884.*

pleasure-ground adjoining Lovers' walk was opened as a place of recreation for the public' (Fig. 18). The site was blessed with a good number of mature deciduous and conifer trees on the southern part and broadleaved trees around the perimeter. Over the next few years the site was further ornamented with a flagpole, a bandstand, additional seats and '12 Iron tablets bearing the words Keep off the Grass in light letters on a dark ground'. In 1885, after the addition of Lovers' Walk, a sub-committee was set up to oversee the management of the trees (Fig. 19).

Fig. 19 Cotham Gardens in their heyday, c1920.

20

In 1889, the new City Forester, Samuel Edward Cockbill set out in his notebook his duties with regard to public parks and gardens. The sites noted are the Pleasure Grounds at Cotham, Bedminster, Hunt's (Mina Road) and St Matthias. His duties were:

1. To keep one proper and efficient man always in the Ground as Caretaker during the periods specified in the Bye-Laws.

2. To provide a substitute Caretaker during a part of Sunday.

2a. Each Caretaker to have 4 days off each Year.

3. To keep the grounds in proper order and all Beds properly weeded.

3a. To provide extra assistance at each ground on Good Friday, Easter Monday and Tuesday and Whit Monday and Tuesday if Surveyor should consider necessary.

4. To prune and cut all trees and shrubs when necessary.

5. To cut the grass when necessary and mow the same once a month if considered necessary by the Surveyor.

6. To supply and plant each Season, Dahlias, Hollyhocks, Sun Flowers or flowers of a like nature of the value of £5-0/0.

6a. Penalty for not putting the ground in order when called upon or not replacing any tree or shrub.

7. To sow flower seeds in the Borders each Season of the Value of £1-10/0.

8. Caretaker to be always provided with cap.

9. If any tree or shrub die the Caretaker to replace at his own cost.

In addition, at Cotham, Cockbill was required 'To plant 1,000 plants in the Flower Beds'.

A good deal of the original layout at the southern end survives intact, with its intricate path system, a good number of mature trees - Corsican Pine, Ilex, Yew - and tufa-lined recesses for seats. Two Copper Beeches flank the southern entrance. Of the Victorian shrub planting little survives, apart from some Laurel and Bay, although a few flowering trees (Malus and Acer) survive. The bandstand has been removed, and the lower part of the park is now dominated by the popular and well-maintained play area. A small wooden arbour shown in early views was sited on the northern boundary looking up the garden.

A winding shrubbery hedge dividing the Gardens from Lovers' Walk survived well within living memory but has now been removed. This boundary was also enclosed with railings now removed. The new railings enclosing the play area are positioned too far east, reducing the size of the Gardens. While the lower garden was always more open than the upper part, its character has been seriously eroded by the development of the play area with its large expanse of hard-surfacing.

ST JAMES'S CHURCHYARD

'For the benefit of the poor of St James's'

St James's Churchyard is a popular, small, city-centre garden. On warm days, it is crowded with office-workers at lunch-times, and offers a vital green cushion to the brutal Bond Street, as well as a glimpse of foliage for the eyes of weary shoppers in Union Street.

Historically, St James's is a fine example of a Churchyard converted to a public garden, a movement which was begun in London under the 1881 Open Spaces Act. The meeting of the Local Board of Health of 15 June 1882 moved for the matter of closed or disused Churchyards and burial grounds to be dealt with 'as had been done in London'. In fact, some parishes had already taken the initiative themselves: the parochial authorities for the Temple Church, St Nicholas and St Philip as well as St James's all turned redundant burial grounds into public gardens around 1880.

In the eighteenth century the Churchyard, now a triangle, was a complete rectangle, with diagonal paths meeting in the centre. However, even at this time, the south-west to north-east path was clearly a much-used informal thoroughfare from Bridewell Lane to St James's Barton, and the future line of Bond Street became increasingly well-established.

Until 1813, St James's Churchyard was unenclosed, but in that year the Vestry applied for a faculty for enclosing the Churchyard, the reason being that, because it was used as a thoroughfare between St James's Barton and the centre of the city, monuments and tombstones were being damaged by 'the many idle and mischievous people passing and hovering there'. The Churchyard was 'becoming a Nuisance and a Scandal to the Neighbourhood'. The Churchwardens also pointed out that valuable land for burials in the city's most populous parish was being lost to 'several useless and unnecessary Paths'.

During the nineteenth century the land south of the cross-path was increasingly used for events such as the St James's Fair and the churchyard as a whole became an important public open space. In 1858, Matthews' *New History of Bristol* referred to 'the parade in St James's Churchyard' as one of the public walks in the city.

The sub-division of the Churchyard by the diagonal path paved the way, literally, for the removal of the

City's hay market from Broadmead to St James's. In 1838, the Vestry agreed to the market's relocation to the southern half of the Churchyard, with a dwarf wall and railing to match that of the rest of the Churchyard. The road to be paved between Bridewell Lane and St James's Barton was made a generous forty feet wide, although no one guessed its growth into the monster that would one day be the modern Bond Street.

By April 1882, the St James's Vestry was anxious for the Corporation to take over their 'newly laid-out' Churchyard. The Vestry's work seems to have comprised levelling and moving tombstones, returfing the ground, building rockeries, planting shrubs and flower beds and providing seats and asphalt paths. The Vestry's request was swiftly agreed to and on 1 July 1882, the *Bristol Times and Mirror* reported the opening of St James's Churchyard on 30 June by the Mayor. The paper reported that it was a small area but much had been made of it: mainly grass with winding asphalted paths, 'prettily and tastefully arranged flower beds and rockeries, and some of the old trees have been allowed to remain'. The layout was by Messrs Parker and Sons and a fountain was projected for the centre designed by the leading Bristol architectural partnership, Foster & Wood. In September a stone cross, with the figures of St James and St Paul in niches, and a drinking fountain, was donated and erected in the eastern part of the garden.

Fig. 20 *Loxton's drawing of the little garden in the Haymarket, sacrificed to the Lewis's department store in 1955.*
[Bristol Reference Library]

When the Mayor opened the recreation ground, he stated that it was 'for the benefit of the poor of St James's', an interesting distinction, and one which undermines the notion of all public parks being places where the classes mingled freely (the Mayor's residence overlooked the Downs, termed 'the people's park' by the *Mirror* on 16 May 1865, but evidently a very different class of people). The Mayor pointed out how fortunate the City was to have the Downs to which people could travel by train, 'but there were doubtless many in the densely populated parish of St James who having to work so many hours, were unable to get to them, and then there were housewives who had family cares, young children, aged people, and invalids, to whom this open space so near to them would be beneficial'.

In 1894 the Haymarket site became the subject of a vehement legal dispute between the Vestry and the Corporation, both sides claiming ownership. After an appeal the Vestry won, and promptly offered the land for building. To save it, in 1896 the Corporation paid £7,500 for the site and a further £2,000 the following year to lay out a public pleasure ground and widen the adjacent streets.

The Haymarket was a public garden for the first fifty years of this century before being built over (Fig. 20). Despite its small size - or perhaps because of it - this was one of the few parks in which bye-laws permitted public meetings. It included a drinking fountain erected by the Merchant Venturers as part of the movement in the 1840s and 1850s to provide drinking water in response to the crisis in public health in the City. The garden was sacrificed in 1955 to allow for the building of the Lewis's department store. As a reminder of this little garden, the statue of Samuel Morley MP survived on the traffic island until the late 1990s, but has recently been removed to the other end

of Rupert Street, to make way for another of the sail-like structures currently popular in the city.

The railings of the Churchyard appear to be quite old, though not in the Bristol style, so presumably were the work of the Vestry. The central walk has now effectively divided the Churchyard triangle into two separate gardens. That to the west has a central path paved with gravestones and good quality new benches. Limes line the central walk, and London Planes are planted along the boundary with the surrounding streets. The central walk is paved in Pennant, with cobbled gutters. In the larger garden there is a quaint tiled gardeners' shelter and store which has recently been repaired. Around the shelter are the remains of a rockery with some quite large lumps of limestone still in place and on the rockery facing the entrance there is what is now a historic City and County of Bristol sign. There is a hexagonal base in the south-west corner of this garden, presumably once the site of a drinking fountain although Loxton shows a seat, now marked incongruously with a central flowering Cherry. The cross has lost its head leaving it a rather undistinguished stump. Along Bond Street, the mature London Planes mitigate the traffic to some extent. In the eastern part of the garden there is a sundial with crazy paving paths centring on it, as well as two unusual stone benches. There are new gates and Bath stone gatepiers on the north side of the garden.

GREVILLE SMYTH PARK

'The People's Park at Bedminster'

Greville Smyth was the first substantial park created by the City in the 1880s. The land at Bedminster had the advantage over Eastville, which had come up as a proposition even earlier, of being a gift. The land in question was the Clift House estate which had been the dower house for Ashton Court used by Florence Upton, sister of John Smyth, until her death in 1852. Her grandson, John Henry Greville Upton, born in 1836, inherited Ashton Court on her death and in that year assumed the name of Smyth. In 1859 Greville Smyth, as he was known, was created a baronet; he was made High Sheriff of Somerset in 1865 and died 27 September 1891.

Although in the early nineteenth century Clift House was evidently quite prestigious, approached by an avenue from just within the Ashton Gate, and commanding views over the river, after Florence Upton's death it seems to have declined in importance. Throughout the 1870s, the Clift House area was mooted as a possible location for the construction of tanks to deodorise the city's sewage and the house itself had been conveyed to the City in 1878, but then on 16 June 1881, the Sanitary Committee recorded receipt of a letter from Stephen Harding, the Smyths' yearly tenant, suggesting that a field of 21 acres would be suitable for making a park for Bedminster.

The Committee considered it a 'very desirable situation ... for the use of ratepayers, and more especially for those living at Bedminster and the Hotwells'. They also reported that they had received a letter from Thomas Dyke, Sir Greville Smyth's agent, saying that he would 'have pleasure in giving the piece of land to the City of Bristol for the purpose of forming a Public Park or Pleasure ground'. It was resolved to accept the gift.

On 12 October 1882, Frederick Ashmead was asked to prepare a layout, and on 13 March 1883 he took the Committee on site to explain his proposals. However on 12 May, the *Times and Mirror* reported on the subject of 'The People's Park at Bedminster' that thirteen different plans 'of varying excellence' were viewed by the Open Spaces Committee for laying out Bedminster park, submitted by 'local and other Surveyors'. This suggests that Ashmead's scheme was not popular with the Committee, but on the other hand it cannot be taken to mean that any of the other thirteen schemes was preferred.

Plate 1 *The lake at Eastville Park: designed on picturesque principles and still a favourite location for boating.*

Plate 2 *Children enjoying the lower pond below Cabot Tower on Brandon Hill, with the original gardeners' kiosk in the background.*

Plate 3 *The paddling pool in St Andrew's Park, a welcome facility on summer days.* *[Bristol City Council]*

Plate 4 *A tranquil scene in St George Park.* *[Bristol City Council]*

ASHTON PARK BEDMINSTER, BRISTOL.

Fig. 21 *Greville Smyth Park as newly laid out, in the early years of this century.*

28

Work began before the final conveyance: fifty new seats were authorised on 25 May 1883, to be supplied by Messrs Jones & Co. for £52. Once the ownership was sorted out, the major investment could begin. On 23 September 1884, work was approved to protect the site from the flooding to which it was prone in winter. In addition the Corporation resolved that the whole length of the land against the public road leading to Ashton 'be fenced with a fence wall and iron railings with entrance gates, that an entrance lodge and tool house be built, that paths be laid out and trees and shrubs planted at a cost not exceeding £3,000'. A month later the contract for laying out and planting the new park was awarded to Messrs Parker & Sons for £1,280 (Fig. 21).

On 5 May 1887, the Sanitary Committee received a request from the Reverend Walter H Fisher of Ashton Gate wishing to erect a drinking fountain in what was known as Bedminster Park. The Committee directed that one similar to that in Cotham Park be provided, the Surveyor to submit a plan for it and for two urinals. A bandstand was erected, identical to those in Cotham Gardens and Mina Road, in 1887 (Fig.22). In 1889 the City Forester's duties were as for St Matthias (qv) but he noted that he had to supply 'Dahlias, Hollyhocks to £5-0/0 and flower seeds £2-0/0' for Bedminster.

Activities in the park in the early 1890s included concerts by the Bedminster Down Brass Band and

Fig. 22 An expansive looking Greville Smyth Park as recorded by Loxton.   [Bristol Reference Library]

Bristol, West of England and the South Wales Operatives Trade and Provident Society's Bristol District Band. Boys from Ashton Gate Board School were allowed to drill in the park. In 1905 the open air pool was opened along with those at Eastville and Victoria Parks. A clubhouse for the bowling green was erected in March 1909 as part of a programme including Eastville, St George and Victoria Parks.

A further four acres to be added to the park was given to the City by Lady Smyth on 23 June 1902, with a request that the park, previously called Bedminster or sometimes Ashton Park, should be re-named 'Greville Smyth Park', a request the City granted. However, the Smyths' development of Frayne Road and Clift Road along either side of the avenue approach to Clift House (c1903-04) removed a slice of the park and eroded its setting on this side, a six-foot high Pennant rubble

Plate 6 The imposing avenue of London Planes in St George Park, on the line of the old Church Walk.

Plate 5 St James's Churchyard, an oasis in the centre of Bristol.
[Bristol City Council]

Plate 7 Sledging in St Andrew's Park in winter.

Plate 8 *Ornamental bedding in Victoria Park.*   [Bristol City Council]

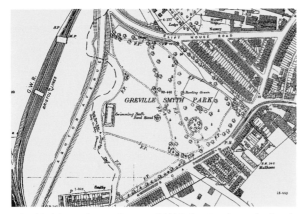

Fig. 23 *The Ordnance Survey of 1918 showing the park already encroached upon by new roads.*

wall being built along the new boundary. At the same time, the construction of Ashton Avenue to the west and between 1903 and 1918 the construction of Clift House Road to the north took substantial slices off the park (Fig.23). Clift House survived as a hospital for diphtheria before being replaced by the bonded tobacco warehouses in 1919. The Cumberland Basin road improvements involved the loss of an additional acre in the north-west corner in 1964.

The park's character has been eroded as much by the dominance of football pitches on the level areas as by the Cumberland Basin approach-roads. At the south-west entrance there is a decent, brick and tiled public lavatory with a cupola. The Ashton Road boundary is a Pennant rubble wall from which the railings have been removed, although a short run survives at the Ashton Road end of Frayne Road. The north corner by Coronation Road and the boundary with Frayne Road are well-stocked with specimen trees and shrubs, including Yew, Cedar, Cypresses, Ilex, Holm Oak, Forsythia and Weeping Ash. The boundary is also marked in the western half by imposing London Planes.

The main entrance is opposite Duckmoor Road, and comprises a pair of central piers with two pedestrian gateways to either side. Just inside this entrance the ground rises steeply and has been ornamented with rockery work and planting. There is now a play area half way up the south-western slope. To the east and south of the bowling greens, there is well-structured formal planting, principally of Limes along paths, but also other mature specimen trees. On top, disappointingly, there is an ugly works compound surrounded by wire mesh, which contained until the early 1990s a little gardeners' kiosk. The sports pavilion is actually rather a striking modernist building, dating presumably from the thirties, although now in dismal condition. There are bits of rockery work on the south-west side of the tennis courts. The straight walk which used to descend to the bandstand survives, lined with quartz and limestone rocks and planted with Limes, but the bandstand has been removed and its place occupied by the large play area.

MINA ROAD PARK

'To elevate the taste of those who live in the neighbourhood'?

This park's history gives an intriguing glimpse of the mixed motives behind what is sometimes now presented as selfless generosity on the part of landowners, and the famous but dubious image of the paternalistic benefactor. No doubt there was a good deal of generosity, but it was also often bound up with self-interest.

The core of the land on which Mina Road Park was laid out was a gift made to the Corporation in 1884 by a Mr William Hunt, a partner in the law firm Hunt, Hodson, Bobbett and Castle, who resided at an elegant villa called Northcote in Westbury. Hunt attached a condition to the gift, that the park be laid out like Redland Grove, by which he must have meant Cotham Gardens. He was asked by the Sanitary Committee to relax that condition but gave two reasons why he was not prepared to do so: 'first to prevent invidious remarks which are now too frequent as to one part of the City being dealt with more liberally than another and secondly that a place laid out as Redland Grove will be likely to elevate the taste of those living in the neighbourhood'. The Committee argued for a layout according to what they considered to be required in that locality adding that 'it would be impossible to maintain an Ornamental Flower Garden in that locality without considerable expense'. It is not clear what negotiations followed, but by the following year, tenders for the work of laying out the garden were being sought.

The eventual cost of the laying out of 'Hunt's Pleasure Ground' as it was originally called was £1,480, and it was opened by the Mayor on 30 June 1886, the same day as St Matthias Park was opened. The design was prepared by Frederick Ashmead, the Borough Engineer, who supervised the work, and also had the contract to supply the seats.

In the centre, two thousand cubic yards of earth were excavated to form a lake. The spoil was spread over the rest of the land raising levels by 12 to 18 inches, a prudent move given the proximity of Cutler's Mills Brook, a tributary of the Frome. An island was formed in the centre of the lake, using between twenty and thirty tons of rock from Cheddar. The brook, which formed the boundary at this date, not only supplied the lake but was ornamented with weirs. In addition, stated the report of the opening in the *Western Daily Press* for 1 July, 'there is a beautiful bed of moss, which gives an apparent depth to the water in the lake beyond that really existing, the actual depth of water

Fig. 24 *Loxton's drawing of Mina Road: the epitome of a well-tended neighbourhood park.*

being only nine inches'. The pond was reported nevertheless to have been well-stocked with fish, and in 1888 water lilies were planted in it.

The *Western Daily Press* report also notes that the new plants 'afford a pleasing relief and the general aspect is improved by the red-berried Cotoneaster'. Other plants noted included Deodar and Atlantic Blue Cedars, Wellingtonia and Japanese Red Cedars, as well as 'other favourite species and the sides of the enclosure are set off with ornamental Trees'.

In 1887, along with Cotham Gardens and Greville Smyth Park, Mina Road received a bandstand. Judging from the applications for permission to use the bandstand it was a popular feature: the Baptist Mills Bible Class Reed and Brass Band, and the Bristol Temperance Society's Reed and Brass Band to name but two were regular performers here. (Despite this popularity, the Council voted against a proposal in October 1898 to meet the cost of providing band music out of the rates.)

On 9 December 1890 the Council agreed to extend the park by purchasing four houses and 'a piece of void land' in Mina Road, originally intended for the development of a new road called Boswell Street. One was kept as a caretaker's house, and it was still in use as such within living memory, although now incorporated in the adjacent hostel. The landlord of these houses was William Hunt and one wonders why he decided at this stage to sell. It seems more than possible that his gift of land and request for the City to lay out a highly ornamental pleasure ground had been made with an eye to future land values; he had hoped that the park would raise the development value of his land adjoining the park and when the Boswell Street development did not happen he decided to pull out.

In its heyday, Mina Road had a full-time park ranger and the park was beautifully maintained. Its paths were 'tar-paved', and Loxton's sketch of c1910/20 shows a neat pond with an island decorated with rockery edging, a railed enclosure, a caretaker's shelter and a neatly trimmed hedge along the backs of the houses in Sevier Street (Fig. 24). The pond is said to have been destroyed during the Blitz, and of course the railings were also removed during the war, although interestingly in 1944 the City found funds to provide new playground equipment.

Mina Road contains one of the most beautiful structures left in any of Bristol's urban parks. The ornate cast-iron urinal in the eastern corner of the park adjacent to Mina Road is listed Grade II. It is no more than typical of Victorian mass-production but now seems, perhaps because of its very isolation, almost a work of art (Fig. 25).

Mina Road is still fronted by imposing London Planes, but without the railings to cap it the dwarf Pennant stone wall is a sad feature. Along Cowmead Walk, the railings have been replaced with chain link on iron stanchions, and clearly such stanchions were also erected at one point along Mina Road. The park's trees comprise an older framework of London Planes, a good Acacia and a notable old Willow (just too far east to have been the same tree which stood on the lake island), with a good deal of later, less structured planting of ornamentals, Norway Maples, Cherries etc. The park has been subdivided to form a popular play area and an area for ball games. The play area includes a large mound at its northern end, the origins of which are not clear.

A good quality timber bridge has been built recently, spanning the brook giving access to the land on the south side of the brook. What appears to be the base of the keeper's kiosk also survives. The condition of the listed urinal is a cause for serious concern: boarded up, its roof fragmenting, the sound of leaking water from within. As one of the few authentic items of Victorian park architecture left in the City, its repair is a matter of urgency. Mina Road Park is now the subject of repair works costing £60,000 developed with local people, including resurfacing of paths, replacing of seats and litter bins. New railings and planting are planned for 2000/2001.

Fig 25 *The urinal in the corner of Mina Road Park; an off-the-shelf structure which now seems architecturally distinguished among the remaining historic park buildings in Bristol.*

36

ST AGNES PARK

The Reverend Wilson's missionary zeal

St Agnes Park is in itself small but needs to be seen as part of a larger philanthropic vision which includes the 1886 church by Wood Bethell (described as 'one of Bristol's best Victorian churches'), the adjacent Mission Hall of 1882 by Charles Hansom, and the lodge. As a group they are a unique illustration of a comprehensive vision of Victorian improvement - paternalistic but also practical - driven through in the face of Council hesitancy and reluctance. The complex relationship between the Council and the enthusiastic 'outsider', in this case the remarkable headmaster of Clifton College, the Reverend James M Wilson who also ran the College Mission in St Agnes, is revealed in fascinating hints and glimpses in the Council minutes.

By the early 1880s little open ground still remained in this crowded, industrial area. The Mission's curate was the Reverend (later Canon) Hardwicke Rawnsley, who went on to help found the National Trust on the basis of Christian socialist principles and concerns for the urban poor. St Agnes was his proving ground, before he moved to the Lake District, and here his sympathies with Octavia Hill were established. The influence of the Reverend Wilson is undocumented but must - given Wilson's energy - have been considerable.

Wilson had been the College headmaster since 1878, preaching muscular Christianity to the privileged, but at the same time establishing the Mission and running it clearly with missionary zeal and concern for the conditions of the urban poor. In 1882, Wilson began his campaign to secure a patch of orchard ground for a public garden, organising a petition to the Council in August. He clearly saw a well-designed and maintained public garden as essential in promoting the spiritual well-being of St Agnes.

His lobbying of the Council was initially met with indifference: he was told that the proposed park in St Andrew's would be quite sufficient provision for St Agnes. But by 1884 the Council had agreed and a year later bought the freehold of the orchard from its owners, the parish of St James's. Wilson had offered to fund the laying out of the park if the Council would undertake its future maintenance, and quickly supplied a plan and bird's eye view but the Council seems to have taken no immediate action. The plan included a lodge with a cloak room, a refreshment room, a retiring room for ladies, and a room for men; a fountain, an ornamental pond, a bandstand, a greenhouse and a summerhouse, two drinking fountains, as well as storage sheds and shelters. Separated from the main

Fig. 26 *A drawing from the Clifton College Mission, showing the Reverend Wilson's vision of St Agnes Park. [Bristol Reference Library]*

ornamental garden by St Thomas Street, the area to the east was to be a playground. In 1884 the Committee responsible for parks was complaining of its lack of resources, and suggested modifying Wilson's scheme; indeed, it queried all Wilson's structural proposals except for a drinking fountain, saying they were not necessary 'at present'.

The correspondence which begins almost immediately after the Council had bought the land in 1884 - with Wilson asking permission to carry out works such as building a lodge and the Council prevaricating - suggests a degree of jealousy on the Council's part towards a well-intentioned and persistent visionary, and its own, more weary 'realism'.

The garden eventually created, largely through Wilson's efforts and to his plan, was an elaborate one. A book produced in 1890 by Clifton College includes drawings of the garden by pupils showing ornamental rockeries, flower beds, ponds and a bandstand (Fig. 26). Wilson was evidently tireless in pursuing donations - a fountain from a Mrs Garnett of Rownham House, rocks from a Mr Charles Thomas, as well as gifts of plants and trees. The lodge, main pond, rockery and mound seem to have been Wilson's own projects.

The Council seems to have gradually warmed to these initiatives, introducing further improvements such as tar paving, a urinal like Mina Road's, boundary shrubs and trees, and appointing a park keeper. By 1898 the City Forester was spending more on flowers for St Agnes than any other public park in his care (Fig. 27).

The park's highly ornamental character has declined quite recently. As late as the mid-1980s it was noted for its shrubberies and rockeries and an ornamental pond in the north-east corner. Only the bare bones now remain of the structure created a hundred years ago. Wilson's fine straight walk, aligned on the west window of St Agnes Church, survives, as does the lodge. The mound at the western end appears to have been regraded and has lost its rock-work and ornamental planting. The bandstand which stood in the separate garden east of St Thomas Street has gone of course,

Fig. 27 Loxton's view of the park confirms its horticultural interest and intricate design.   [Bristol Reference Library]

although that area still retains its original function as a playground. Decisions to remove features such as the ponds and horticultural displays to reduce future maintenance have drastically changed the garden's character. Other decisions, such as the planting of the diagonal row of Cherries, have blurred its design. However, this is still a valued neighbourhood park: in 1996 a memorial garden to the community leader, Evon Berry, was created in the north-east corner, and the survival of the main structure of the park means that much could be done to make this once more a green lung in a still densely built-up residential area.

EASTVILLE PARK

The battle for a park for St Philips

Eastville Park occupies an important place in the history of urban parks in Bristol. The acquisition of the land was the subject of a long-running campaign for a park for the over-crowded and unhealthy parish of St Philips and was the focal point of political debate over the wider need for public parks in a self-respecting city. After the arguments of the 1870s reached a stalemate, as described in the Introduction, the case for purchasing the land at Stapleton was resurrected again by a populist campaign. This was probably due to the feebleness of the Council's provision of open space in St Philips in the intervening years. This comprised the churchyard of St Philip and St Jacob, the ground around Lawford Gate Prison, and Gaunt's Ham Park, for the small size of which the City felt obliged to apologise publicly.

After the acquisition of Gaunt's Ham in 1887, the Bristol Operatives Association held a series of public meetings and then formally lobbied the Board of Health, while the Liberal MP and Councillor for St Philips, Mark Whitwell, raised the matter again with the Council. Another site inspection by the Authority's Surveyor, Frederick Ashmead, followed and finally

Fig. 28 *A Loxton view of Eastville Park, showing the formal walks and one of the characteristic little shelters erected in many of Bristol's parks.* [Bristol Reference Library]

a site of 70 acres was bought from Sir John Greville Smyth for some £30,000 in January 1889.

The park was laid out to a plan by Ashmead although he complained about the task being outside the terms of his contract. It was situated on what was then the edge of late nineteenth-century Bristol and there were originally doubts, hard to imagine today, about its remoteness. The land was hedged but well-treed, with a steep bank of woodland overlooking the river. To convert it to a park, the City took out the hedges but kept the mature trees, repaired the existing boundary walls and laid out paths with a hundred seats and several small wooden shelters (Fig. 28).

Fig. 29 *A fascinating Loxton drawing of work in progress on the enormous earthworks involved in constructing the lake.* [*Bristol Reference Library*]

41

Walks were created using structural planting of Limes (now partly replaced with Horse Chestnuts) and London Planes. The grass was managed with both sheep grazing and mowing. That basic provision was augmented over the next three or four years with a caretaker's lodge, refreshment pavilion, bandstand, drinking fountains, a urinal; the swimming pool followed in 1905, the bowling greens in 1907, and the lake in 1908-09. The first boathouse was burnt down, reputedly by suffragettes, in 1913, as was its replacement, with the present one having been built in 1925.

Eastville and Windmill Hill were two of the few sites where land was allocated in the bye-laws for the holding of public meetings. The omission of a general right of assembly in the new parks was highly controversial: on 23 June 1891 the Bristol Labour Emancipation League sent a resolution, strongly protesting at the proposed interference by the Corporation with 'the rights of the Citizens of Bristol to hold public meetings in their large parks' and the Bristol Socialist League also protested emphatically 'against any restriction of the Citizens' undoubted rights to hold public meetings in our large Parks and Public Spaces'. In Eastville meetings were allowed, but only by prior consent of the Sanitary Committee. It was the need for this consent that infuriated labour groups and others: a motion was put to the Local Board of Health on 14 July 1891 after the Gas Workers and General Labourers' Union had submitted a petition proposing to rescind the bye-laws but it was lost 16 to 24.

Almost all the approaches have been compromised by road-encroachment: the widening of Fishponds Road in 1909 involved cutting back the Park for nearly the whole of its frontage on the road, resulting in the still crude embankments on much of this frontage. The M32 took the lower entrance, with its walls, gates and drinking fountain in the 1960s (Fig. 11). The best entrance is probably the north-west corner, which takes you in under the remnants of a fine clump of London Plane and rewards you with a prospect of the park stretching out below.

Across the scorching plains of the playing fields and down the steep hanging wood on Pennant-finished steps, you come to one of the best public park lakes in the country. Constructed by hundreds of unemployed applicants to the Distress Committee's Labour Bureau in 1905, in what had been a water-meadow, it is designed on perfect picturesque principles (Fig. 29). Serpentine in form, its boundaries hidden so that from no point can you distinguish its exact size, and bordered by lawns, specimen trees and the hanging wood, it is a wonderful feature. The earthworks on the western and southern sides are substantial and still sharp, making a highly impressive landscape (Fig. 30).

Fig. 30 The lake at Eastville, arguably the best landscape feature in any Bristol park, and little changed today.

Fig. 31 The remains of the drinking fountain in Eastville Park.

There is fine planting around the lake, for example the group of Beech east of the concrete shelter, and those on the lower slopes of the bank.

The park has lost most of its original built features. The bandstand had gone by the middle of the twentieth century. The little kiosks have also long gone. Only the plinth and footings of the octagonal drinking fountain by the Fishponds Road entrance still survive, with a stand pipe which no longer supplies water (Fig. 31). The Crimean War cannon which stood on a plinth near the bowling green, pointing towards Eastville Boys' School across the road (demolished c1990), was removed during the second World War.

The swimming pool - three walls at least - survives and was made into a community garden by the Avon County Council Environmental Scheme in the early 1980s. So does the boathouse and its very popular boats. The run of railings on a dwarf Pennant wall along Fishponds Road is probably the best in Bristol, although the run extends for less than half of the wall's length, and the wrought-iron gates on Fishponds Road are in a later style. The park has many of its original rustic cast-iron benches, although the row solemnly ignoring the park to look instead at the M32 is one of the more bizarre bits of park management in the City. The bowling greens are still much enjoyed and play an important role in the social life of the local community.

The sports use of the central western area has resulted in the felling or non-replacement of one of the major lines of trees in the original park. The view across this area is now fairly bleak as a result. Late twentieth-century additions which do not do much for the park include the sports pavilion and the pair of concrete shelters, one by the lake and the other by the sports pitches.

VICTORIA PARK

A rival to Durdham Downs

The 1845 Report on the Sanitary Condition of Bristol stated that the worst conditions in what by 1850 was recorded as the third most unhealthy city in England were in the four oldest parishes. These included Bedminster, where a dense population had been established in the first half of the nineteenth century. Pressure grew steadily for a park in south Bristol, and although Victoria Park was not included in the first group of public parks and gardens reported in 1884 (Greville Smyth Park was of course), on 19 January 1887 there was a report to the Local Board of Health that the City Surveyor was investigating a piece of land on the 'southward side of the Great Western Railway, between St Luke's Road and Windmill Hill' and trying to find out who the owners were.

On 9 August 1887, the Sanitary Committee reported to the Local Board of Health that the land on Windmill Hill which comprised 37½ acres could be bought for £350 per acre, concluding 'Your Committee consider that this piece of land affords a very desirable site for a Pleasure Ground'. The *Bristol Times and Mirror* report on that meeting spoke of the eager response to buying this land. Councillor Davies had itemised the advantages: on three sides was a dense population; 'It was easily accessible from all parts and would be as much a park for Redcliffe as for East Bedminster' - an exaggeration that rankled in St Philips - and 'So far as the views were concerned they rivalled the Durdham Downs and it would be especially appreciated by the working classes'.

The paper's editorial for 10 August endorsed the proposal although it warned that 'it remains, in fairness as well as in expediency, that the needs of the East end of the city should be taken into consideration. It should be bourne (sic) in mind that this is not only a question of amusement and recreation, but also one of health. It is important that, in every city, especially in a growing city like Bristol, some spaces be kept open which can never be built upon. Delay in such matters may be dangerous. The land, for instance, at Windmill Hill would be built upon in a few years time, in the ordinary course of things'.

With public and Council support the Committee went ahead with the purchase and preparation of a plan by the City Surveyor. The transfer of the bulk of the land, 39 acres from the trustees of Sir John Greville Smyth, was made in May 1889, with the other parcels acquired soon after. In all, 51½ acres were acquired for a total of £20,678.

Windmill Hill had long been a place of public resort and also a place for public meetings: in 1887, the Committee had received a request for a drinking fountain there. And on 20 September 1888 a resolution from the Meeting of the Ratepayers reported to the Committee suggests something of the conflict underlying the gentrification of this tract of land: 'This meeting desires to call the attention of the Sanitary Authority to the extensive use of the land on Windmill Hill, and trusts that an endeavour may be made to hasten the purchase of the same in order that it may be brought under proper control, and that those who are so anxious to enjoy the use thereof shall have the right to do so'. Significantly the same group also urged that the land's name be changed, to Victoria Park.

Ashmead's plan met with approval and on 23 May 1889, he was asked to prepare a specification and estimate for laying out Windmill Hill in accordance with the plan produced and already approved. He also went ahead with letting the tenders for the initial work: drainage, forming paths, removing hedges, erecting temporary fences, walling, planting and so on. In August, the Liberal Councillor for Bedminster, William Terrett, presented a drinking fountain of his own design, depicted in many views of the park (Fig. 32).

Progress on Victoria Park was swift compared to other parks. A bandstand was erected in March 1890 and a

Fig. 32 *Loxton's drawing of the drinking fountain in Victoria Park.*
[Bristol Reference Library]

ranger, Mr John Cleak, was appointed in April, when the Open Spaces Committee made a site inspection. *The Western Daily Press* of 14 April reported on the visit and said the councillors were pleased with progress: 'The need for a recreation ground in the neighbourhood was shown by the large number of children making use of the park at the time of the committee's visit'.

Despite progress, money was obviously tight for the Council as on 13 October 1891 authorisation was sought from the Local Government Board for a loan of £7,200 for providing entrance gates, seats, urinals, shelters, etc., and for planting, laying out, and fencing Windmill Hill, Eastville Park, St Andrew's Park and Gaunt's Ham. The Committee stated that they 'are now of the opinion that by an increased expenditure the appearance of the Parks may be considerably improved, the access thereto made more convenient, and better accommodation provided for the public as regards fountains, shelters and urinals'. Approval came through in April 1892 and more contracts, for dwarf walls, gate piers, gates and railings were promptly let.

The creation of the park spurred on the developers who owned the neighbouring land. From 1891 the Smyths, William Vowles and George Pearson all developed streets around or near the park. Nutgrove Avenue is a good example of the kind of higher quality housing which could be introduced given open views over a public park. The construction of the schools in 1885 probably coincided with the first expressions of interest in laying out Windmill Hill as a park.

The expanse of grass posed problems for management, and after receiving only one tender for a mowing contract, the Committee let the park for grazing for three years at £50 per annum, restricting the stock to sheep.

By 1897, the City Engineer could report that 'Victoria Park, Bedminster, has been very much improved by the erection of iron fencing to flower beds and shrubberies, and by the laying of tar paving beside 372 yards of gravel paths laid where the gradient is too steep for tar ... Swings, see-saws and horizontal bars have been erected in this Park, which are in constant use and much appreciated by the public'.

By 1898 the park had four permanent rangers. As well as the bandstand, its features included two drinking fountains and a Crimean cannon sited near the Somerset Terrace entrance (Fig. 33). There was a railed circular pond inside the St Luke's road entrance. An open air pool was built in 1905 at the same time as those at Eastville and Greville Smyth Parks, but was demolished after the second World War. Between 1905 and 1918 tennis courts and a bowling green and even a quoit ground were added. The layout too continued to develop: for example, the cannon, once acquired, was made the focal point of new straight paths including a second east-west route; and the north-western part of the park, above the old Rope Walk beside the railway, was planted up, perhaps in order to screen the new vicarage. Flower beds were laid out inside the western entrance between the gates and the cannon, ornamented with rockeries (Fig. 34) and 'stumperies' (constructions of upturned stumps with flowers planted among the exposed roots) were also created here (see Fig. 33).

VICTORIA PARK, BEDMINSTER, BRISTOL.

Fig. 33 *The Crimean War cannon at the Somerset Terrace entrance with a stumpery on the right.*

The park has lost some important elements of its planting, such as the trees that were massed around the entrances on Hill Avenue and the perimeter planting along this road, although the surviving London Planes are impressive. The railings along this fine boundary wall have also been removed. Where the south side of St Luke's Road was demolished it has been replaced with a newer Pennant stone wall with concrete caps. The path system has been simplified throughout the park, and the feeling of an overall structure has been reduced. The huge curved double row of what seem to have been Limes round the bandstand, recorded in 1905, seems already to have been thinning out by 1918; the best bit of formal tree-planting remains the double row of Limes along Nutgrove Avenue, although incomplete in places now.

All the free-standing built features have disappeared: the urinals, the drinking fountain, the cannon (although the stand of the lamp which stood beside it survives), the bandstand, and the pool. However, the complex of school buildings, retaining walls and steps on the north side is a remarkable piece of townscape, despite the absence of railings along the school boundary. From the site of the cannon the eastward walk is lined with Robinia, and there is also a good group of London Planes at the end of Vivian Street. The Somerset Street entrance still has the keeper's lodge and four gate piers although its gates are missing.

Fig. 34 *Flower beds and dwarf fencing clearly made Victoria Park a place to be proud of.*

Modern features include the pond and wildlife area near the children's play equipment and, much more interesting, the water maze designed by Peter Milner and Jane Norbury and built by ACCES and the City Engineers department in 1984. The design is based on one of the roof bosses in the church of St Mary Redcliff, water is supplied by a spring on Knowle Hill and it was built to mark the end of sewage discharge into the River Avon. This is a notable addition to Bristol parks in recent years, genuinely in the spirit and character of the municipal ornamentation and a real pleasure to users (see page 61).

ST ANDREW'S PARK

'Leisurely action on the part of the city authorities'

St Andrew's Park is the classic neighbourhood park, laid out at the same time as the designed housing development which now surrounds it. Twenty-two acres were offered to the Council as early as 1882, by Mr Derham, of Derham Bros., boot manufacturers and developer of the St Andrew's estate, on the 'highest and healthiest part of the estate'. However, its cost at £550 per acre was high and the Council declined the option on offer. Instead they went ahead with Bedminster, which of course was a free gift. Sustained pressure principally from the local ratepayers' associations resulted finally in the purchase of half that area at the end of 1890 for the purpose of creating 'a People's Park for Bristol North'. The Council also agreed to contribute to the developers' costs of laying out the roads around it.

The area had been used for quarrying and was considered a beauty spot largely because of its elevated situation, and there was some opposition to its being formally laid out as a park. The Council tipped a great deal of rubbish and spoil from surrounding building works to level the uneven ground but progress was

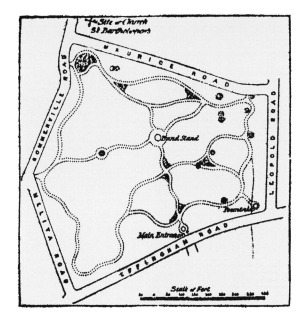

Fig. 35 *The original plan of St Andrew's Park as recorded at its opening in the Western Daily Press, 2 May 1895.*

slow, even though work began in advance of both the final purchase and a design. The Committee authorised the purchase of 30 seats in August 1890, and on 15 June 1893, still two years in advance of its formal opening, the Bishopston Total Abstinence Society was granted permission to hold meetings in the park subject to the Surveyor's directions. In April 1892 fencing 'similar to that at Cotham Gardens' was approved but the tender was not let until October.

Fig. 36   A beautiful photograph showing the ornate layout within the park and its railings and boundary planting.

Evidently the local residents were impatient with the lack of progress and on 1 March 1894 the Sanitary Committee received a memorial from the Ratepayers of Bristol North 'requesting the Authority to at once lay out St Andrew's Park and appoint a caretaker to enforce the observance of the bye-laws'. In May, a caretaker was appointed, a Mr J Harris who was to be paid 22 shillings per week. In April the Surveyor was asked to submit 'a design and price for a stone fountain'. The total eventually spent on the layout was £6,190.

Fig. 37 St Andrew's Park in an undated, early postcard.

Finally, in May 1895, the park was ready for its formal opening. The design, by Frederick Ashmead's successor, Mr C F Ball, divided the park into two distinct areas: the lower area was laid out as 'an ornamental pleasure ground' and the higher, northern area was reserved as a place 'where young people will be able to amuse themselves to their hearts' content upon the green sward' (Fig. 37). The whole was bounded with dwarf walls and railings, with a perimeter belt of shrubs (Fig. 36). A bandstand and a drinking-fountain in red and grey granite were erected, paths were tar-paved, island shrubberies and flower beds at the junction of the many paths were planted. The Ratepayers' Association had already made arrangements for three band concerts a week.

The press reported a variety of reactions - some felt that 'a plain park and not the dressed up white elephant we now have' would have been preferable, and bemoaned 'the poor taste in filling up with thousands of loads of rubbish the beautiful undulating paradice (sic) nook of nature'. One correspondent complained, 'What entrancing shelter from the wind and sun the west corner would afford if it had been laid out with shrubs, as the configuration was left by nature's hand.' In fact the land was not natural, having been quarried, but the decision not to capitalise on the former quarry as an ornamental feature may well have been the result not of aesthetics but of the revenue generated by the tipping. In place of the rough ground and sheltering hollows there were railings and 'Keep off the Grass' notices. But others praised the City's design as well as the park's natural advantages, its 'wide panorama' over Kingsdown, Redland and Westbury Park, and its contribution to the health of the surrounding population: 'there is nothing', reported the *Western Daily Press,* 'to hinder the western breezes from the Channel reaching St Andrew's Park with scarcely diminishing freshness.'

The *Bristol Times and Mirror* added that the history of the park was one of 'leisurely action on the part of the city authorities'. For three years after its purchase the land had remained 'cut up and uneven, the depository of much of the rubbish that had been used in the building operations that had been carried on, and also of most of the old tins and such encumbrances of which the residents in the immediate vicinity desired to rid themselves'. The City, the paper asserted, had been spurred into action by the vigorous lobbying of the St Andrew's Park Ratepayers' Association.

Further developments followed with the bowling greens laid out in the 1920s and a range of glasshouses large enough that by the early 1960s St Andrew's, with Blaise and Oldbury, was one of the City's three principal suppliers of plants for the Corporation's parks as a whole, producing over 25,000 plants a year. In 1950 a water tank was converted into the children's paddling pool and the new brick pavilion was built later that decade dwarfing the attractive 1920s timber structure.

The park remains very well-used with its original catchment area still intact and prosperous, but most of its built and planted features have disappeared (Fig. 38). The shrubberies and stumperies shown in early postcard views have gone, although the Corsican Pines around the perimeter remain from the original boundary planting. There is a good group of Horse Chestnut near the drinking fountain, and a fine group of three London Planes. A number of specimen trees and structural planting (chiefly Limes) along the paths survives, and vestiges of the ornamental shrub and tree planting in the lower area survive, including an Atlantic Blue Cedar. Around the site of the glasshouses, where the present

Fig. 38 *The bandstand has gone, but the loss of railings and shrubberies has had an equally drastic effect on the park's character.* [Bygone Bristol]

yard is located, there are remnants of shrubbery planting including Laurel, Holly, and Box.

The bandstand is thought to have been removed in 1946; the railings went during the war and the imposing drinking-fountain has been replaced with a stand-pipe which no longer works. Only the circular foundations remain of a sundial sited between the main entrance and the south-west corner. But the basic structure of winding walks remains, and the mature tree-planting around the perimeter and along the paths is still substantial.

ST GEORGE PARK

The making of a suburb

St George Park has the strongest design of any of Bristol's parks, and this may be because it was the responsibility not of the Corporation but of the St George Urban District Council. Less wealthy than the City, it was however outside the hegemony of the slow-moving Sanitary Committee and its surveyor.

In 1860 the parish's open land was largely devoted to market-gardening for Bristol's growing population. But over the next thirty years there was 'an explosive outburst of building energy' over Totterdown, St Philip's Marsh, Easton and St George. By 1897, when it was incorporated in the City, most of St George as we know it today had been built. Whitehall Colliery stood just off the present Lake View Road, and high slag heaps stood where Lyndale Road and Sloan Street now run.

In the 1890s, civic amenities started to develop: the Grade School in 1894, the public library, a gift of the Wills family, in 1898, and the St George Picture House in 1899. Part of this investment in the public realm was the acquisition in 1894 of Fire Engine

Farm for the purpose of laying out a public park. The farm was largely treeless (unlike the Eastville land) and the farmhouse stood where the present lodge was built. The park was crossed by public paths, including a well-established east-west route known as Church Walk, which eventually was incorporated in the avenue. The land was watered by the Wain Brook which flowed westwards across the site.

A park had been mooted as early as 1890 when Handel Cossham MP, the leading Liberal and Nonconformist colliery owner who had campaigned for better mass education, and who organised and gave popular classes on mining engineering, expressed the hope that he would be able to provide the district with a public park, saying there was a need for a park to bridge the long distance from Eastville and Windmill Hill. He suggested land near his residence Holly Lodge, between Deep Pit and Speedwell Pit, 'an exceedingly pretty spot, the attractions of which have been in course of improvement for some years past by planting of trees and the addition of artificial water' (*Western Daily Press*, 4 April, 1890). However, Cossham died unexpectedly soon after that speech and left no mention of a park in his will.

Unlike Eastville, St George was consciously planned to be the centrepiece of a new suburb with its own civic identity and character. The farm had belonged to the Church Commissioners, and its 38 acres cost the Local Board £12,000. This was argued to be less than half its development value, and certainly it was considerably less than the price asked by the Smyth family for the land at Eastville.

After an informal opening in July that year, with fireworks, a banquet for dignitaries and buns for the children, a design competition was announced with competitors including the leading garden designer, Thomas Mawson. The winning design was actually by the borough surveyor, T Lawrence Lewis, but the competition approach seems to have produced a higher specification and level of expectation on the part of the Council than we see generally among Bristol parks. Mawson was evidently put out at not being chosen, and a Park Committee minute records that in October he was asking that 'as the designs were not to be acted upon they may be returned'.

The design for the park is much more sophisticated than any of the other urban parks in Bristol with its combination of axial paths focussed on the bandstand, and its elegant serpentine circuit walk. The park contained both formal and informal elements in its planting and, unlike Eastville, the lake was integral to the design (Fig. 39). Judging by the design's quality, Lewis probably did, as Mawson evidently feared, lift some elements from the latter's plans.

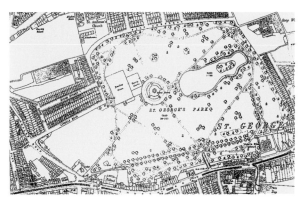

Fig. 39 Ordnance Survey plan of St George Park, 1918: a comprehensive design.

In October, Lewis submitted estimates for the cost of laying out the park, which included laying out the path network, culverting the brook and constructing the lake, building the bandstand, the lodge, shelters, kiosks and urinals, lighting and fencing, and the Board sought sanction from the Local Government Board for a loan of £6,500.

In the autumn, work began on grubbing out the old hedgerows and fencing the park boundary. Then in the spring, estimates were requested by the Committee for tree and shrub-planting, making specific mention of Lime, Horse and Sweet Chestnut, Rhododendron, Birch, Box, Holly, Black Poplar, Hawthorn (red and white), Laburnum, Lilac, Barberry, Sycamore, Azaleas and Laurustinus. The Committee seems to have taken a close interest in the project, even going so far as selecting the sites for the individual trees. In September 1896 the Surveyor was asked to provide a sketch of border planting, for which a Mr W Smith supplied shrubs for £90.10s.6d.

For the structural planting, the same nurseryman proposed heavy standards for the trees, the Poplars being 12-foot stems, the Limes, Chestnuts 10 feet, the Hawthorn 8 feet and the Sycamore, Laburnum, Birch, Maple and Plane between 6-8 feet. The shrubs too were also well grown-on, the lilac being 4-5 feet high, and the others around 2-4 feet. A dozen of each tree and shrub was ordered. Horse Chestnuts were decided upon for the avenue, to be planted 60 feet apart and at 60-foot intervals.

In April the Committee advertised the post of caretaker or ranger. Wages were to be 21 shillings per week with a uniform included; hours were 8 a.m. to 8 p.m. weekdays and 10 a.m. to 8 p.m. Sundays 'with the exception of about 2 hours on Sunday afternoon'. Within a fortnight, thirty applications had been received. The Committee agreed that only applicants from the parish of St George would be considered, and after interviewing four candidates, the Committee appointed Robert Clements to the position. In September, the Committee agreed to give Clements alternate Sundays off.

A urinal was built on the site of the present public lavatories near the school, in November 1896, and the Committee asked the Surveyor to find out the cost of supplying a shelter for the park-keeper. Incredibly, it took a Committee resolution on 7 December to allow the poor man to wear his Fire Brigade overcoat.

By the winter of 1896/97, the Committee was having problems. The lake was leaking, and the contractor was proving difficult, especially as the Committee had insisted on providing the clay for puddling. On 14 December, the Committee asked him to repair the leak, but he denied responsibility. His contractual maintenance obligations expired on 1 January, and the problems continued. The Committee received reports on the rate of leakage - 16 inches in 10 days according to the Surveyor on 22 February, and the Surveyor was asked to make an inspection to locate the leak.

The Committee also had to put up bills offering a reward of 20 shillings for anyone giving information that would lead to a conviction of offenders damaging trees. In February the chairman, Albert Verrier, had recorded: 'I fear that from apparent trespass on the beds they must be fenced with continuous iron fence about 200 yards long'. Mr Smith, the nurseryman, was also causing problems. In December, he revised his estimate for the shrubs downwards in response to a complaint from the Committee and in February

Fig. 40 *A postcard dated 1909 showing the completed park.*

Fig. 41 The Victoria Free Library, designed by Sir Frank Wills; the original covenant on the Fire Engine Farm land had to be amended to allow building in the park. [Bristol Reference Library]

Verrier remarked that 'The ivy plants on banks at Church Road entrance are not planted according to my idea'. In March, Smith had to be asked to replace dead trees. The unregulated use of the park for football, even at night, was damaging the turf; there were continuing disputes over the boundary with neighbouring owners.

But struggling progress on the works continued. In February, it was reported that the walk up Place Avenue to the bandstand was under construction and the mound for the stand was nearly completed; planting of the lime avenue to Whitehall gate, presumably from the bandstand mound, was to

proceed. Mr Smith was to plant the island with 'rose trees'. In May, the wall round the lake was completed and the footpath asphalted, the main entrance finished, two shelters and a ranger's hut were built and 'a footway 10 ft. wide to be constructed down to the bandstand mound, using up Cemetery stone for foundations' - the bandstand was 'to be erected if anything left'. Money was clearly tight: a request from Mr Clements for advance of his wages was deferred for two months at the meeting of 5 May. There was sufficient however to memorialise Lewis and the Board's Clerk, Joseph Stubbs, with plaques on the main gate piers, the first dated 1896, the second 1897.

Later in 1897, the City took over the functions of the St George Local Board. The City Engineer's account in his report concluded 'This park still requires a large amount of outlay'; of the four hundred and fifty new trees in the park, for example, barely a hundred were alive. On 6 July 1899, the Council borrowed a further £7,000 to replant Mr Smith's failed trees and shrubs and to finish the laying out, including replacing the main avenue's Horse Chestnuts with the present London Planes.

By March 1902, the work had been completed: paths tar-paved, nearly four acres of plantations, comprising over ten thousand deciduous and evergreen trees and ten thousand flowering shrubs, supplied by Messrs

Garaway and Co. The avenue of Planes was replanted, the bandstand erected, along with two drinking fountains, and two urinals. Five flights of artificial stone steps were constructed, the banks of the lake were shaped and sown with gorse and broom seed, and about a further eight acres of ground were Ztilled and sown with grass seed (Fig. 40).

The park remains fundamentally unaltered: there are no significant incursions by building and its main structural features are still in place, principally the lake and the London Plane avenue. The loss of Sir Frank Wills's Victoria Library, demolished in the 1970s, was however most regrettable not only because it was a fine building in what Gomme and Jenner termed 'a dainty Jacobean' style (Fig. 41) but also because its cheaply made little replacement fails utterly to complement the park and school as part of the civic amenities of St George. There were drinking fountains at two entrances, one at least of the same circular pattern as that at Eastville; they too have gone. The bandstand (Fig.42) was removed in 1958; its octagonal shape is still discernible on the mound up which steps still rise. The bowls pavilion features some elegant iron work and must date from the 1908 laying out of the green. Like Eastville, St George Park had its cannon, sited directly inside the main entrance and presumably removed at the same time as the Eastville gun, during World War II.

Fig. 42 *The bandstand in its setting: a big loss to the park.*

The main entrance at the junction of Church Road and Chalks Road is a commanding piece of the streetscape with its Pennant ashlar piers with memorial tablets to Lewis and Stubbs, and its red brick lodge. However, the gates have been removed and the lodge appears to have been either rebuilt or much re-worked. The surviving piers, gates, railings of St George Library all survive and are listed. Loxton's drawings show low railings round the lake and a mixture of railings and iron post and rail fences along some paths and around shrubberies, all now removed. (Fig. 43)

The western area of the park, beside Chalks Road, has been appropriated for car-parking. Although never an intensively ornamented part of the park, it was used as a playground and as a public meeting place. Its change of use means that the new, large skateboard area intrudes further into the park than otherwise necessary.

Some of the surviving clumps of London Plane are particularly well sited. Apart from the Avenue, other good trees include Lime, Ash and Acacia in the southern perimeter belt, a couple of Deodar Cedars, and some Holm Oaks at the eastern end of the park. The walk from the gates to the bandstand was always open, but as a feature there were clumps at its junctions, now removed. On the other hand, Leyland Cypress planted at the northern end of the tennis courts threaten to overwhelm the balance of tree-planting as they shoot skyward.

Fig. 43 *One of Loxton's many drawings of St George Park, showing the low railings around the lake.* [Bristol Reference Library]

CONCLUSION

After many years of neglect and a downward slide in the list of Council priorities, parks across the country seem to be on the verge of a renaissance. The Heritage Lottery Fund has poured over £150 million into them in the last four years and continues to budget £30 million per year to its Urban Parks Programme. A House of Commons Select Committee has recently published a passionate report on the need for good public parks. Central Government may gradually be acknowledging their importance.

Bristol has secured multi-million pound grants from the Lottery towards restoration projects in Queen Square, Blaise Castle and Ashton Court. While the Lottery cannot redress the problems of all Bristol's parks, we must hope that its evaluation of the importance of those open spaces may awaken our councillors to the social, environmental and economic benefits of well-maintained public parks. Parks were the first item in the Leisure Services Department Annual Report for 1999, and the Department has carried out research identifying parks as one of the key reasons that people value the city as a place to live. The Lottery grants have pushed parks back up the political agenda and it seems as if the Council is at last recognising its responsibilities to its citizens, who make 16 million visits a year to their local parks. If this book can contribute to a renaissance in Bristol's parks then it will have done its job.

Water maze in Victoria park - see page 49

Acknowledgements

Special thanks to Colin Young, who as at Weston has preceded me through the Council minute-books and who generously shared his notes; thanks also to the Avon Gardens Trust, the staff of the Bristol Record Office, the Bristol Reference Library, and the City Museum and Art Gallery, to Stewart Harding, Peggy Stembridge, and Peter Wilkinson.

Imperial measures have been used throughout this book. You may find the following conversions useful.

> 1 inch = 2.54 cm
> 1 foot = 30.48 cm
> 1 yard = 0.914 m
> 1 mile = 1.609 km
> 1 acre = 0.405 hectares

Although inflation prevents any direct comparison, our pre-decimal currency included old pennies, of which there were twelve in one shilling, which is equivalent to five new pence, and there were twenty shillings to one pound.

Further Reading

Clifton College, *The History of St Agnes Parish 1876-1890* (Bristol, 1890)

Hazel Conway, *Public Parks* (Princes Risborough, 1996)

Madge Dresser ed., *The Making of Modern Bristol* (London, 1995)

Stewart Harding and David Lambert, *Parks and Gardens of Avon* (Avon Gardens Trust, 1994)

David Lambert, **'The Parks Movement in Bristol'**, Avon Gardens Trust Newsletter, 18 (Spring 1997)

John Latimer, *The Annals of Bristol in the Nineteenth Century* (vols.3-4, 1887 and 1908, repr. Bath, 1970)

H E Meller, *Leisure and the Changing City, 1870-1914* (London, 1976)

J F Nicholls and John Taylor, *Bristol Past and Present*, vols.1-3 (Bristol, 1881-82)

Iris Royston ed., *Redfield and St George of Yesterday* (1950)

St George Townswomen's Guild, *A Short Thesis on the History of St George* (c1978)

G F Stone, *Bristol as it was and as it is* (Bristol, 1909)

Reece Winstone, *Bristol as it was* and other volumes (38 vols. to date, Bristol, 1957 onwards)

Colin Young, **'The Making of Bristol's Victorian Parks'**, Transactions of the Bristol and Gloucestershire Archaeological Society, 116 (1998), pp.175-84

Avon Gardens Trust Publications

Parks & Gardens of Avon

The former County of Avon has splendid historic parks and gardens, both urban and rural, which brilliantly illustrate the history of gardening and landscape parks in England. This profusely illustrated book provides an important and fascinating record of the historic development of these landscapes.

ISBN 0 7291 0230 0   1994 132 pages £7.95

Thomas Goldney's Garden

Thomas Goldney, a Quaker merchant, created this eighteenth century garden, which survives today in Clifton. This booklet tells of the building of the famous grotto, the planting, the gardeners and the visitors who left accounts of what they saw. There are contemporary illustrations and maps, in black and white and colour.

ISBN 0 9518290 2 5   1996 30 pages £3.50

Historic Public Parks

These two books on Historic Public Parks of Bath and Weston-super-Mare are companions to the present volume. The origins and development of the parks are described, and there are maps and contemporary illustrations. The books are equally interesting to read at home or to take on a walk round the parks.

Bath	ISBN 0 9531013 0 4	1997 76 pages	£5.95
Weston	ISBN 0 9531013 1 2	1998 56 pages	£5.95

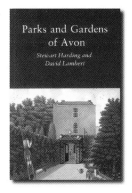

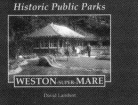

All available from good bookshops or direct, post included, from Avon Gardens Trust, CREATE Centre, Smeaton Road, Bristol BS1 6XN